A Jerry Baker Home Hints Booklet

Clean It Up!

120+ Secrets to Keep Your Stuff in Tip-Top Shape

Don't abandon your belongings just because they've lost their luster. With the quick and easy tips and tricks in this book, you'll give your grubby goods a whole new lease on life!

You might think that some of the items we're about to discuss seem kind of odd: After all, who bothers to clean a curling iron? But once you've spiffed up your stuff, you'll realize that everything looks better, works better, and feels a whole lot better when it's clean. And be sure to follow up with my *Fantastic Finish* ideas. They'll keep your things in fine fettle for good.

You'll find plenty of super solutions that'll get your stuff clean—without using harmful chemicals. In fact, most of the ingredients in my *Fast Formulas* are already right inside your kitchen cupboards.

So what are you waiting for? Get ready to bust the dust, and clean up these terrific treasures:

- **Air Conditioners**
- **Bathrooms**
- **Cameras**
- **Christmas Decor**
- **Curling Irons**
- **Dehumidifiers**
- **Dolls**
- **Electric Mixers**
- **Electric Shavers**
- **Exercise Stuff**
- **Fans**
- **Fruits & Veggies**
- **Gutters**
- **Hair Dryers**
- **Hats**
- **Hearing Aids**
- **Humidifiers**
- **Kitchens**
- **Laundry Rooms**
- **Litter Boxes**
- **Mirrors**
- **Toys**
- **Velcro®**
- **Waffle Irons**
- **Wicker**
- **Yard Tools**

For more of my terrific tips, tricks, and tonics, check out my website, **www.jerrybaker.com**. It's packed with plenty of how-to information to keep everything in your home, yard, and garden in tip-top shape!

Air Conditioners

1 **A monthly date for a filter check**—Cleaning the filter is the easiest maintenance you can perform on your air conditioner—and your allergies! The more dust you keep from entering the system, the better it is for both your airways and your equipment. So check your A/C filter once a month, and if it's clogged with dust, slip in a new one (or wash it, if it's the reusable kind).

2 **The key to a longer life**—Once it's rinsed clean, here's a quick and easy way to extend the longevity of your filter: Tape a piece of cheesecloth to the outside of it. It'll catch gobs of filter-clogging lint, hair, and dust.

3 **Don't "leave" it alone**—Make cleaning leaves and pine needles out of your A/C unit part of your annual spring cleaning routine. Remove the cover, then use your shop vac to get the big stuff, and a vacuum cleaner with a soft bristle brush attachment to clean out any other debris.

4 **Focus on the fins**—While you're at it, remove the side grids, and use a soft brush to clean the aluminum fins. Finish up by hosing them down, making sure you point the nozzle to the outside of the unit so you don't drown the motor.

Safe and Sound

The aluminum fins are sharp to the touch and easy to bend, so be very careful—only use gentle up-and-down strokes to clean them.

5 **Rinse and reuse**—Most window air conditioning units come with a reusable plastic filter. To clean it, just slide it out and give it a quick rinse with a hose, then pop it back into place.

Bathrooms

6 **So long, soap scum!**—Make that cloudy layer disappear from your bathroom's tile in a jiffy. Just sprinkle a little baking soda on a damp sponge, rub away the film, and then rinse thoroughly to remove all of the residue.

7 **Rejuvenate your tub**—The next time you clean your white porcelain or fiberglass tub, follow up on the scrubbing with a good, long soak: Fill the tub with hot water, and drop in several denture-cleaning tablets. Let it sit overnight, then rinse it clean in the morning. Now that's a bright, shiny finish you can smile about!

8 **From fridge to faucet**—Believe it or not, an ordinary bottle of ketchup will work wonders to clean your bathroom's brass or bronze faucets. Just squirt a big dab onto a dry cloth, and rub it over the faucet until all of the grime is gone. Then rinse the faucet and buff it dry.

Fast Formula

This quick and easy all-purpose cleaner makes it as easy as pie to keep your tub, shower, and tile looking like new:

- 3 cups hot water
- 1/2 cup vinegar
- 1 tablespoon dishwashing liquid
- 1 tablespoon borax

Mix all of the ingredients in a handheld sprayer bottle, and give it a good shake. When you're ready to tackle the tough spots, just spray 'em down, and then wipe the cleaner (and the crud) away.

9 **Color-coded**—If you regularly use yellow rubber gloves to clean around the house, how about a purple, green, or blue pair for toilet duty? That way, they won't get mixed up with your regular cleaning gloves and spread nasty germs to other parts of your home. Store them under the bathroom sink.

10 **H-2-low**—When it's time to clean your toilet, make it easier by lowering the water level in the bowl. Just pour about half a bucket of water all at once into the bowl. Then push your bowl brush quickly in and out of the exit hole. Finally, shut off the water to the tank at the pipe, flush, and the toilet won't be able to refill.

Safe and Sound

When a cleaner containing ammonia is mixed with one that contains bleach, the result is a deadly chlorine gas. So never mix any kind of cleaning products together.

11 **Put it on automatic**—Make a medium-thick paste of automatic dishwasher detergent and water, lower the water in the toilet bowl, and apply the paste. Close the lid, let it sit for about 15 minutes, and swab the bowl. Stains will vanish—automatically!

12 **Take two tablets**—Drop in two Alka-Seltzer® tablets to clean a toilet bowl from the water line down. Close the lid for about 20 minutes, then brush away the loosened crud.

13 **Tangy tip**—Citric acid makes a great toilet bowl cleaner. Simply drop 2 teaspoons of Tang® or powdered lemonade mix into the water. Let it work on the stains overnight, then the next morning, just brush and flush!

Cameras

14 Handle with care—Cameras and camcorders are amazing workhorses, considering how complicated their inner workings are. But dust and dirt can really throw a monkey wrench into those innards, and that's when they need help. So before you even think about doing-it-yourself, dig out the owner's manual, read up on the recommended care, and follow all directions to a T.

15 Body cleanup—Unless your camera is made to go under water, always keep liquid away from it. Just use a dry microfiber cloth to wipe off dust and an artist's paintbrush to get to the lint that accumulates around the buttons or other crevices.

16 Better contact—Keep your camera or camcorder humming along by removing the batteries after every use and cleaning the contact points with a pencil eraser. Rub any dirt away, and blow the residue into a wastebasket.

17 Air alone—As you wipe your camera clean, be sure to keep the cloth away from the fragile lens. Clean it with the power of plain old air instead! Just blowing on a camera lens or camcorder viewfinder will do the trick, or use a can of compressed air to blast the dust away.

For a Fantastic Finish...

Here's an easy way to protect your fragile camera lens from dust, dirt, and fingerprints that can eat into the coatings: Add a transparent lens cap filter over the top of the lens. For about $20, it's the best—and cheapest— insurance policy your hard-earned money can buy!

Christmas Decor

18 Santa's sack—Save yourself the hassle of vacuuming up piles of needles by placing a tree disposal bag underneath the stand before you set up your live Christmas tree. The giant-sized bag can stay neatly out of sight until it's time to slip it over the tree and haul it to the curb—without dropping a single needle!

19 Winter windstorm—If you're not sure if your artificial tree is washable, keep it away from water. Tackle the dirt with the brush attachment on your vacuum that's been covered with a layer of cheesecloth. Set it on "low," and run the brush over the branches.

20 Shower time—To freshen up a washable Christmas tree, give it a quick shower before you put it away. Disassemble your tree, and swish the branches in a tub filled with water. Shake any excess water away and let the pieces air dry for a day or two.

21 Thin-skinned—A light swipe with a dry microfiber cloth will restore Christmas tree ornaments' shine. But leave hand-painted or antique decorations alone or you could damage the finish.

22 Practice your art—When your glittery ornaments are looking a little dusty, brighten them up with a soft artist's brush.

23 Air 'em out—Hang several dusty ornaments on a drying rack in your garage, and give 'em the once over with your blow dryer set on cool. They'll be ready to dazzle in no time at all.

Curling Irons

24 **Cool it!**—Make sure your curling iron is unplugged and completely cold to the touch before you start cleaning it.

25 **Swipe it with alcohol**—Hair care products make a mess of a curling iron. So wipe yours with a cloth dampened with isopropyl alcohol.

26 **Steel yourself**—Once the gunk is gone, a rub-down with steel wool will leave your chrome curling iron sparkling clean.

27 **Foam it in**—Tackle burned-on styling products with foam oven cleaner. Just spray the rod of the iron with the cleaner, let it sit for 30 minutes, and rub the dirt off with a plastic scrubbie.

28 **Finishing touch**—Whichever cleaning technique you use, wipe the iron afterward with a damp cloth to remove any residue.

Fast Formula

Tackle extra stubborn residue on your curling iron with this old softie:

1 tablespoon of liquid fabric softener
1/4 cup of warm water

Combine the ingredients in a small bowl, then rub the mixture onto the stains with a cotton swab. Wait about 10 minutes for the gunk to loosen, and then wipe it away.

Dehumidifiers

29 **Monthly maintenance**—Wash the water container in your dehumidifier monthly to keep it fresh. Remove the reservoir, scrub it inside and out with a soapy sponge, and then rinse and replace it.

30 **Condense the cleanup**—A $10 appliance condenser brush will clean the coils without damaging any delicate parts. And it's not just for dehumidifiers—it'll clean the coils on refrigerators, too!

31 **Filter finder**—Check your owner's manual to see if your machine has a filter; if it does, give it a rinse once a year.

For a Fantastic Finish...

Your dehumidifier is like a small refrigerator, right down to the fans and coils that keep things pumping along. The problem is that those hard-working parts can get mighty dusty, even if your machine has its own filter. Here's how to keep it humming:

1. Every six months, unplug the machine and remove the panels that hide the inner parts. Drop the screws into an ice cube tray, separating them by kind and color.
2. Use the crevice tool of your vacuum cleaner to gently suck up the dust that's hiding inside the machine.
3. Clean the coils and fins with a soft brush.
4. Wipe the fan with a soft, dry cloth.
5. Reassemble the unit, and you'll be good for another six months of hard-working service.

Dolls

32 Scrub the surface—Spruce up vinyl dolls with a soft cloth dampened with mild dishwashing liquid and water. Use your cloth-covered fingertip to gently stroke away any dirt from the doll's bodies and faces. Get between the fingers and toes with a cotton swab dipped in soapy water.

33 Clean your face, dolly—To wash a stain off a doll's vinyl skin, mix cream of tartar with lemon juice, dab it on the spot with a cotton swab, wait about 30 minutes, and rinse thoroughly.

34 The eyes have it—To clear the blinking eyes of old plastic dolls, put a drop of sewing machine oil on a cotton swab, and wipe the eyeball. Use a light touch, so you don't nudge the eyes askew, or push them out of their sockets.

35 Blemish free—If you can't wipe an ink stain off a doll's skin, smear a dab of acne cream with 10% benzoyl peroxide on the mark. Wait about 2 hours, then rinse it off with a clean, damp cloth.

For a Fantastic Finish...

Washing modern doll clothing is as easy as caring for your own full-sized duds: Put the tiny attire into a mesh lingerie bag, toss it in your washing machine on the gentle cycle, and run it through the dryer on the cool setting. Or you can wash the clothes by hand in warm, soapy water.

Cleaning gets much more complicated the older your doll and her outfits are. If your doll is an antique, limit your efforts to a gentle dusting, or take it to a pro who will have the right know-how for restoration.

Electric Mixers

36 Easy clean—Get the batter off your electric mixer's beaters by whirring them in a bowl of hot soapy water. Then just pop them out, rinse them under hot running water, and let them air dry.

37 Finger zinger—Unplug the mixer before you clean the housing because whirring your fingers in the blades would be no fun at all!

38 Quick wipe down—Spiff up the mixer housing by wiping it down with a damp cloth. Use a toothbrush to scrub out grime between the controls and in the vents. And do a quick swipe of the cord in case the batter splattered.

39 Surface scrub—If stuck-on crud won't budge from your mixer, sprinkle a little baking soda on your damp cleaning cloth.

For a Fantastic Finish...

Your white standing mixer may be performing perfectly, but if it's taking on a dingy yellow "patina," this'll clean it up so you can keep it on the counter:

1. **Dab a paste of baking soda and water onto a microfiber cleaning cloth and scrub the entire surface of the mixer.**
2. **Rinse the machine with a damp cloth, and if it still looks yellow, scrub and rinse it until it's white again.**
3. **Finally, bring back the shine by wiping the clean machine down with a solution of one part vinegar and one part water, and dry it with a soft, clean cloth.**

Electric Shavers

40 **Keep your head above water**—Most electric shavers are water resistant, but not waterproof. So unless your owner's manual says otherwise, never submerge your electric shaver in water to clean it.

41 **Blow it away**—Keep your shaver razor-sharp by blowing bits of whiskers off the head every time you use it. Every few shaves, go a little deeper and dig debris off the blades. Just remove the head, and whisk the blades with the small cleaning brush that came with the shaver. If you've lost the brush, you'll find a replacement in the aisle near the shaving cream.

42 **Grease the wheels**—Most electric shavers need an occasional dab of head lubricant to keep their metal parts running smoothly. So once a week, spray the screen lightly with the lube while the shaver is running; you'll hear a tone change as it works its way through the system.

43 **Dip off the dirt**—When the cutting block of your electric shaver gets grungy with a greasy buildup of bits of hair, skin, and body oil, give it a bath. Just remove it from the shaver, dip it in a bowl of warm, soapy water, and wipe away the grime.

For a Fantastic Finish...

It can be mighty tempting to give your electric shaver a tap on the sink to make those tiny whiskers fall out, but don't do it. You might just dent the combs or knock them out of alignment, and that can spell big trouble: It's the combs' precision line-up that lifts the hairs so the blades can slice them off. Talk about a close shave!

Exercise Stuff

44 **Don't sweat it**—Wipe down your exercise equipment every time you use it because that salty sweat can eventually corrode the metal or other movable parts. So grab a damp cloth that's got a few drops of dishwashing liquid on it, and wipe perspiration off of the seats, handlebars, and anywhere else it ended up.

45 **Smooth sliding**—Inspect your exercise equipment's movable parts every couple of weeks and wipe any debris away.

46 **Mind that monitor**—Dust off a machine's monitor with a clean, soft cloth. Then spray the cloth with a spritz of my sanitizing wipe (below) to clean off any wayward fingerprints and other grime.

47 **Change your shoes**—To cut down on the crud that accumulates on your exercise equipment, keep a separate pair of gym shoes to wear only when working out indoors.

Fast Formula

Mix up a batch of this sanitizing wipe to use whenever your exercise equipment needs a quick cleaning. It'll cut through grime and kill germs at the same time.

1 part isopropyl alcohol
4 parts water

Mix the ingredients in a handheld sprayer bottle, and keep it handy. Then spray it on, and wipe it all away.

Fans

48 **Blow it away**—When dust builds up inside of your electric fan, give it a few shots of compressed air to blow the gunk away. Don't aim the nozzle at the motor, but at the crud that collects in the center of the fan where the blades attach to the drive shaft.

49 **Clean the screens**—To remove the dust that collects on your electric fan's protective screens, unplug the fan, take the screens off, and wash them in warm, soapy water. And while the thing's unplugged, dampen a cloth with a little vinegar and wipe the fan blades clean. Once the screens are dry, reassemble the fan, plug it in, and enjoy the clean breeze!

For a Fantastic Finish...

Sock it to your ceiling fan and give it a deep cleaning that'll remove built-up grime. Here's how:

1. Fill a handheld sprayer bottle with my secret ceiling fan formula—white vinegar!
2. Spread a drop cloth on the floor under the fan, and set a sturdy step stool on it.
3. Get 2 or 3 old white cotton socks—yes, I said socks—they're super for cleaning your ceiling fan.
4. Spritz the first fan blade with a little vinegar, slip a sock onto your hand, and wipe off the dirt.
5. Repeat the procedure on the other blades and the motor, turning the sock as you work so you're always wiping with a clean part. Toss the dirty sock onto the drop cloth when you're done with it, and switch to a new sock whenever the old one gets too grimy.

Fruits & Veggies

50 **Be firm with germs**—Research shows that most bacteria and dirt are trapped near the ends of fresh fruit and vegetables, where the blossom fell off or the stem was attached. So before you wash that zuke or cuke, slice off—and dispose of—the ends.

51 **Clean greens**—Soak salad greens in a large bowl filled with cold water, 4 tablespoons of salt, and the juice of a whole fresh lemon. Let them sit for about 5 minutes, then rinse 'em under cold water.

52 **Easy handling**—Put small fruits or veggies into a colander and set it in a large bowl filled with a solution of equal parts white vinegar and water. Let the colander soak for about 5 minutes, lift it out, and rinse your food clean under cold running water.

53 **Baking soda scrub**—Wash waxy fruit or veggies, then sprinkle on a little baking soda, and use a damp paper towel to rub the coating off. Rinse each piece thoroughly when you're done.

Fast Formula

Keep a bottle of this germ-killer handy to clean smooth-skinned fruits and veggies:

- 1 cup of white vinegar
- 3 cups of water

Mix the vinegar and water in a handheld sprayer bottle and spritz your fruit or veggies with the solution, count to 10, and then rinse it off under running water.

Gutters

54 **Make a date**—Ignoring clogged gutters can cause serious damage to your house if water seeps into the walls or erodes the foundation. So clean 'em twice a year—once in late spring, and again in late fall. Then you can relax and enjoy the soothing sounds of rain on your roof, knowing that your gutters are doing their job.

Safe and Sound

Move the ladder as you work or you'll stretch beyond your reach and could lose your balance. And never hang on to a gutter or downspout because they can let loose with the slightest pull.

55 **Down with debris**—You'll need an extension ladder, work gloves, and a garden trowel to remove the built-up gunk. Hang a plastic trash bag from your ladder with an S hook to dump the debris into as you work. Start at one end of the house, and work your way around the roof, scooping out gunk as you go. When the crud is gone, flush the gutters with a garden hose until the water runs freely through the downspouts.

56 **Super scooper**—Make your own gutter scoop by recycling a plastic laundry bottle. Start with a handled bottle that is no wider than your gutters. Standard 100-ounce bottles should fit just fine. Rinse the bottle out, and replace the cap, then turn the bottle so the handle is facing up, and slice off the bottom at an angle with a pair of scissors. The cut should be angled so the bottom of the scoop is much longer than the top, so cut the top back nearly to the handle. That's all there's to it! Your scoop is ready to slide along the inside of the gutter, scraping up all of the leaves and debris in its path.

Hair Dryers

57 **Just venting**—Your hair dryer has two grilled openings for air. One draws it in and the other blows it out. When either gets clogged your dryer may overheat. So if you see stuff trapped against the grills, sweep it away with an old dry toothbrush.

58 **Extra power**—To remove a linty buildup from your hair dryer's grills, nooks, and crannies, blast it with a shot of canned air.

Safe and Sound

Don't clean or dismantle your dryer while it's still plugged in, or you might have a shocking experience!

59 **Swab it matey!**—For caked-on grime, dip a cotton swab into isopropyl alcohol, and rub the built-up grunge away.

60 **Soapy soak**—Your hair dryer's attachments can get gunked up with styling products, so give them a bath every now and then. Just squirt some dishwashing liquid into a sink full of warm water, and let them soak for about 10 minutes. Wipe them with a sponge or soft cloth, rinse the suds away, and let them air dry completely before you reattach them to the dryer.

61 **Stop overheating**—There's a built-in thermostat on your hair dryer that makes it shut off when the motor overheats. And why does the motor overheat? Because there's dirt clogging up the works, of course! So if cleaning the grills doesn't do the trick, take out the screws that hold the body together, and use a can of compressed air to blow any dust away.

Hats

62 **Stick to the spots**—Most of the time, a simple spot cleaning will be all you need to spiff up your baseball caps. Just rub the cap with a washcloth that's been moistened in soapy water. Then wipe it with a clean, damp cloth and let it air dry.

63 **Dish it out**—A cloth baseball cap will end up a misshapen mess if you throw it in your washing machine, so wash it in your dishwasher instead! Set your cap on top of a plastic strainer that's about the same size. Then set a second strainer on top of your hat, and fasten it to the first strainer with twist ties. Set your "hat sandwich" in your dishwasher, and run it through a cycle.

64 **Give wool caps a hand**—A cap made of wool will shrink it into a matted mish-mash in the washing machine or dishwasher, so wash it by hand instead. Swish it through cool water and a mild soap like Woolite®, then set it on top of a coffee can to air dry.

65 **Get in shape**—Here's a quick trick to bring a misshapen straw hat or wool fedora back into line. Simply boil a pot of water, and hold the bent part over the steam for a few minutes. As the creases relax, bend your hat back into shape, then let it air dry.

66 **Take that, Panama hat**—A real Panama hat sure looks classy—except when it starts to get dirty. Keep yours clean by using a nail brush to scrub it with a mix of castile soap and warm water. Rinse it in fresh water, and pat the hat with a bath towel to soak up the excess moisture. Then dry it on a clean towel in the sun.

If you'd rather not have to break it in again, simply add 1 tablespoon of glycerin to a gallon of water, and use that as a second rinse before you set it outside to dry.

67 **A fine fedora**—When it's time to spruce up a structured hat, like a man's fedora, or a winter hat made of wool felt, brush the surface in one direction all the way around the hat to remove the loose dust and lint. Pay special attention to the crevices around the hat-band and the seams, where dirt likes to hide.

68 **Leather and suede crusade**—Try to avoid getting your leather or suede hat wet, but if it should happen to rain on your parade, shake off the water, and let it air dry away from heat, which can shrink the leather. Rub leather moisturizer onto your smooth leather hat after it dries to keep it supple and gleaming. And brush your suede chapeau to raise the nap after it has gotten wet.

Fast Formula

To clean your straw hat, start by washing the sweatband with a brush dipped in soapy water, then rinse it with a damp cloth. Rub away any stains with this straw hat scrub:

For light colored hats:
- 1 teaspoon of hydrogen peroxide
- 1 teaspoon of water

For dark colored hats:
- 1/2 teaspoon of ammonia
- 1/4 cup of water

Mix the ingredients in a bowl, and rub the dirtiest spots first. Then wipe the entire surface with the mixture. Rinse with a moist cloth and let the hat air dry.

Hearing Aids

69 **Add a toothbrush to your tool kit**—Wiping your hearing aid with a soft cloth when you remove it will keep the outside clean—but it's what's inside that counts, because that's where earwax builds up. So use a soft toothbrush to brush off any wax that accumulates in and near the end of the tube, where it fits down into your ear. A nightly cleaning will keep the crud from settling in, and you'll hear better, too.

70 **Behind the ear**—If your hearing aid is the kind that fits behind your ear, disconnect the non-electronic ear mold from the electronic part, and set it into a bowl of soapy water for a few minutes. Rinse it off, wipe it dry, and blow out the tubing to make sure no water is left behind.

71 **Open door policy**—To make your hearing aid batteries last longer, open the battery compartment door every night when you put it away. That'll allow air to circulate, so that damaging moisture doesn't build up inside the battery case. And if there's any gunk in the case, loosen it with a pencil eraser.

For a Fantastic Finish...

When earwax builds up and blocks the sound outlet port, your hearing aid may distort sound, or only let it through in short bursts. If the buildup is bad, the earwax clog may even cut off the sound altogether.

For a foolproof trick that'll keep the sound flowing freely, consider buying a small vacuum cleaner that's specially made for hearing aids. It'll suck the gunk out in just a few seconds, and make cleaning out those nasty clogs a real breeze!

Humidifiers

72 Crud prevention—Keep your humidifier hummin' along by dumping out the water every day to prevent mineral deposits from settling in the tank. Then wipe the tank dry before you refill it with fresh water. This will get rid of any crud that might start forming inside.

73 Deposit deterrent—Tap water contains minerals that can harden into deposits on your humidifier no matter how often you change the water. If you notice mineral buildup in the tank, switch to using only distilled water. The distilling process filters out the minerals, and leaves you with nice, clean steam.

74 Take off the tank—To dissolve built-up minerals in the tank, unplug the unit, disconnect it from the filter and the base, and fill the tank with either white vinegar or a mix of cool water and a tablespoon of chlorine bleach. Let it soak for about 30 minutes, so the acid can dissolve the mineral stains. Then rinse the tank thoroughly until there's no smell before you refill it.

75 Filter flush—Some humidifiers have a filter that traps minerals and other particles in the water. Check your owner's manual to see where the filter is located, and change it per the manufacturer's recommendation. To coax the crusty minerals out of the filter, soak it in a large saucepan that's filled with equal parts of white vinegar and water. Let it sit for about 30 minutes to dissolve the minerals, and use an old toothbrush (if necessary) to scrub out any stubborn crud. Rinse the filter thoroughly, reassemble your clean machine, and it's ready to go.

Kitchens

76 **Throw in the sponge**—Kitchen sponges start to smell bad after a while, as nasty bacteria move in and make themselves at home. But if your little stinker is still in good shape, don't toss it out! Toss it into your dishwasher instead. The soap and steam will freshen it up and knock any creeping crud dead.

77 **What's cookin'?**—When food spills over onto the bottom of your oven, pour some salt on it. It'll reduce the smoke if you're still baking, and make it easier to clean up the spill once the oven cools.

78 **Scratch removal**—Your glass-topped kitchen table will look like new again if you remove the scratches with a compound called jeweler's rouge. Clean the tabletop first, then apply the compound

Fast Formula

Use this formula to wipe and shine countertops, appliances, windows, and other hard glossy surfaces.*

1 part white vinegar
1 part water

Mix the ingredients in a handheld sprayer and shake it before using. Then spray it on, and wipe the grunge away; there's no need to rinse because the sharp vinegar scent will dissipate as it dries. Keep this wipe on hand indefinitely in a cool cabinet.**

*If your kitchen has marble countertops, don't use this cleaner! The acid in vinegar—even in a drift of spray—can permanently damage your precious stone.

** To clean windows or mirrors, add 2 or 3 drops of dishwashing liquid to the mix.

according to the directions on the label. Wipe off the excess, and let it sit in the scratches until it dries. Then clean the tabletop again to bring out the shine. Jeweler's rouge is available at craft shops or online for just a few dollars.

79 **Melted plastic**—When a plastic bread bag melts on your hot toaster or stove burner, let the surface cool, then saturate a cotton ball with nail polish remover, and rub until the melted mess comes off. Rinse the area clean with plain water.

80 **Don't get grout-chy**—To remove stubborn stains from the white grout in your tiled kitchen counter or backsplash, dab on a bit of foam shaving cream, and let it sit for about 30 minutes.

81 **Streak-free stainless**—Hot pans and hard water leave streaks and spots on your stainless steel sink, and they're tough to scrub away. Rub 'em away instead with a bit of olive oil on a soft cloth.

82 **Baking cupboard confidential**—To remove stains from your porcelain sink, wet it down, then liberally sprinkle it with baking soda. Scrub the surface vigorously in small circles, then rinse well. If any stained areas remain, cover them with a paste made of baking soda and water, wait about 30 minutes, and scrub again.

83 **Kitchen scrub**—Cut through grease and grime on your kitchen counters, floor, and appliances with a mixture of 1/4 cup of baking soda and 1/2 cup of white vinegar in 1 gallon of hot water. Rinse the areas thoroughly afterward to remove all traces of baking soda residue, which can dull the shine.

84 **Yell "oh!"**—Molecules of kitchen grease that go airborne when you cook can leave a yucky yellow film on your nice white kitchen appliances. So when your refrigerator, microwave, or stove start to look a little dingy, mix up a solution of 1/4 cup of baking soda with 3 cups of water, rub it on the surface with a nonabrasive scrubbie pad, and rinse the yellow away.

85 **Finish with a clean sweep**—Don't even think about cleaning your floor until you're done with the rest of your kitchen. You're going to spill stuff as you clean other areas, and you'll probably walk through those spills, too. When it's time to tackle the floor, sweep first, then work toward the door as you mop, so your nice clean floor can dry footprint-free.

For a Fantastic Finish...

Kitchens can get pretty smelly, what with all the cooking that goes on. But you've got an ally when it comes to taming odors—baking soda. For a kitchen that smells as clean as it looks, use these air-fresheners:

- ✓ Keep your kitchen trash can free of foul odors by sprinkling a little baking soda under the trash can liner. Replace the baking soda with a fresh layer about once a month to make sure it stays potent.
- ✓ Foods in your fridge can absorb each other's odors, so keep an open box of baking soda in there. That'll keep your cheesecake from smelling like last night's leftovers! Stir it every week to keep a fresh layer on top, and replace the box monthly.
- ✓ Park an open box of baking soda under your kitchen sink to get rid of lurking musty odors.

Laundry Rooms

86 **Dust bunny bye-bye**—Tiny specks of dust build up fast in your laundry room, collecting in places you'd never usually dream of wiping. So once a week, give the room a thorough going-over. Run a dust mop under the washer and dryer, too, to round up any dust bunnies that are hiding under there.

87 **Efficiency expert**—Clean the insides of your washer and dryer just before you throw in a load of laundry. Wipe out the inside of the dryer with a damp cloth, focusing on the lint that collects around the door. Then rinse and reuse the same cloth to wipe out the washer's tub and the bleach and fabric softener spouts. Add that dirty cloth to your load of laundry, and start the cleaning cycle all over again!

For a Fantastic Finish...

Getting lazy about lint costs you money because your dryer has to work harder and run longer when the lint screen is clogged. So limit lint with these everyday tips:

✓ To remove lint from the screen, wet your fingertip, peel it off, and drop it in a nearby trash can.

✓ Remove lint that collects on the dryer door and gasket.

✓ Wash sweatshirts and towels separately from other laundry because they generate lots of lint. Clean the screen during their drying cycle to keep your machine working most efficiently.

✓ Keep in mind that lint buildup can lead to a fire—so don't ignore this potential hazard!

Litter Boxes

88 **Put a lid on it**—Your house will smell a whole lot better if you use a litter box that has a cover on it. The cover will keep your cat's business out of sight—and out of smelling range! Slip a charcoal filter into the cover to cut down on odors even more.

89 **Stop litter in its tracks**—Keep your cat from tracking a trail all over the house by setting a washable kitchen mat outside of its litter box. The rug will catch any particles of litter still clinging to Fluffy's paws when she steps across it, keeping the area clean.

Safe and Sound

Take a pregnant pause, and don't clean the cat box if you are expecting, or you'll risk coming down with toxoplasmosis, a virus that's dangerous to pregnant women. Take a break from scooping duty, too, and washing the box. Play it safe—let someone else in the family handle the job for now.

90 **Baking soda magic**—Sprinkle baking soda over the bottom of your cat's freshly cleaned litter box before refilling it. Baking soda will absorb a lot of noxious odors, and it won't cause your cat to avoid the box like some chemical scents will.

91 **Scoop and scrub**—Scoop your cat's litter box at least once a day. If you use clay litter, replace the litter at least once a week; for clumping litter, make it every 2 to 3 weeks. After you dump the litter, scrub the box with a hot soapy rag, rinse it out, and spray the box with a solution of 1 cup of chlorine bleach in 1 gallon of water.

Mirrors

92 **Easy cleaner**—A damp cloth works great for regular mirror maintenance. But to cut through smudgy fingerprints or speckles of toothpaste, mix a solution of equal parts vinegar and warm water.

93 **Breaking news**—Crumple a sheet of black-and-white newspaper and dip it into a bowl of white vinegar. Rub the grime off your mirror with the newspaper, then polish it with a lint-free cloth.

94 **Paper problem**—Paper towels make handy cleaning rags, but don't be tempted to use them on your mirrors. Use a soft microfiber cloth instead for a crystal-clear, lint-free reflection.

95 **Sticky situation**—If your mirror has a spot of adhesive residue from a price tag or tape, wipe it away with waterless hand cleaner. Just dip a clean cloth into the cleaner, and rub the mess away.

Fast Formula

Take gunk off your mirror with a few quick swipes of this simple cleaner.

- 1 cup of isopropyl alcohol
- 1 cup of water
- 1 tablespoon of white vinegar

Pour the ingredients into a handheld sprayer bottle. Spray the formula onto a microfiber cloth, and wipe the dirt away. That's all there is to it. Shine on!

Toys

96 **Green clean—** Spritz white vinegar on a cleaning cloth to wipe down plastic and vinyl toys.

97 **Double duty—** Pour a bit of isopropyl alcohol on a paper towel—or better yet, use a disinfectant hand wipe, which is mostly alcohol—and wipe away germs, dirt, and ink stains from plastic, vinyl, or metal toys.

Safe and Sound

Keep dust mites from taking up residence on stuffed animals, or your child may have an allergic reaction. How? Once a week, put the plush toys in a plastic bag and place it in your freezer overnight. It'll ice 'em out for good so you can all breathe a whole lot easier.

98 **Bleach bath—**Disinfect germy toys with a solution of 1 to 2 teaspoons of bleach in a gallon of hot water. Rinse the toys, and let them air-dry.

99 **Erase stains—**To clean a plastic kiddie activity table, or other large piece, wet a Mr. Clean Magic Eraser®, squeeze it out, and gently stroke the toy.

100 **Pool and bath toys—**Wipe slimy, scummy water toys with a mix of 1/2 cup of baking soda in 1 quart of water.

101 **Scrub-a-dub—**When hard plastic or soft vinyl toys start looking grimy, scrub the dirt off with a paste made with 3/4 cup baking soda and 1 tablespoon of water. Use a toothbrush to get at the grunge, then rinse the toys to remove any residue.

Velcro®

102 **Hook the hooks**—The hooked side of a Velcro fastener gets dirty fast because the tiny hooks grab on to anything that passes by. So clean the hooks with—are you ready?—another piece of Velcro! Just slide a clean piece through the fuzzy fastener, and it'll draw off the debris.

103 **Flaps down**—Always take a few minutes to close Velcro fasteners securely before you put a garment in the wash. This little trick will keep the hooks from picking up lint and fuzz.

104 **The cat's meow**—The thin metal bristles of a cat brush are just the right size to get into Velcro hooks to loosen the lint. After a few quick strokes, the sticky strip will be fuzz-free.

105 **Stick to it**—Press a piece of packing or duct tape firmly against the hooked side of a velcro fastener, and peel off the crud.

106 **On a roll**—Velcro hair rollers work great, until they get covered in hair. To shed the problem, rub two rollers against each other, then use a small crochet hook to snag the loosened hairs.

107 **Tool time**—If you have kids with Velcro clasps on their clothes, you'll be doing a lot of lint-picking. So why not invest in a tool that makes short work of the chore? The handy GripClean® device, made especially for cleaning self-stick fasteners, is easy to use, and it only costs about $5 at drugstores.

Waffle Irons

108 **Pull the plug**—Be sure the waffle iron is unplugged and cold inside and out, before you clean it up and put it away.

109 **Sticking solution**—If your waffles are sticking, you may be opening the lid too soon, or not using enough oil in the batter. Use rubber tools to remove the stuck-on bits; metal will scratch the surface and lead to more sticky situations.

110 **Stay away from the spray**—Don't spritz a non-stick waffle iron with cooking spray, or grease the grids with cooking oil or the extra oil will build up a gummy residue.

111 **Batter up!**—Never submerge a waffle iron to clean it. A damp cloth will handle any wet spills on the appliance and the cord.

112 **Oil the slide**—Soak dried-on batter with a few drops of cooking oil for 10 minutes, and then rub the iron clean with a damp cloth.

For a Fantastic Finish...

Waffle irons with metal grids are usually pre-seasoned at the factory. If your grids haven't had the treatment, here's how to season the iron yourself:

1. **Pour a little cooking oil onto a paper towel, wipe the grids, and heat the iron until it begins to smoke.**
2. **Go ahead and bake a waffle, but don't eat it.**
3. **The next waffle will be perfect. And the oil in the batter will deepen the seasoning every time you use the iron.**

Wicker

113 **Bust the dust**—Wicker is a real dust catcher, so go over it regularly with the upholstery attachment on a vacuum cleaner.

114 **Sunny day shower**—Set wicker porch furniture in a shady spot to sponge it down with soapy water. Let it air dry.

115 **Protect the paint**—If wicker is painted, a good thorough dusting will take care of most of the dirt. For a more thorough cleaning, whip up a bowl of frothy suds to wipe it down.

116 **Mildew matters**—Remove dark mildew stains with 1 cup of chlorine bleach in a gallon of water. Scrub the stained area until the spots are gone, then rinse it with a clean, moist sponge.

For a Fantastic Finish...

When wicker or other natural fiber baskets need more than just a dusting to look their best, try one of these tips:

- ✓ Wipe sticky, greasy film away with a solution of 1 part white vinegar and 1 part water.
- ✓ Wash dirty fingerprints and other smudges off with a soapy sponge. Use a cotton swab to reach into the nooks and crannies, and rinse with a damp sponge.
- ✓ Rub stubborn spots with baking soda on a damp cloth, or dab it with a cotton ball soaked in lemon juice.
- ✓ Take neglected baskets outside and slosh them with a wet, soapy sponge, then rinse them off with a garden hose.

Yard Tools

117 Gardener's secret—Gardening is messy business, and trowels, weeders, and other tools can quickly get caked with soil and mud. So spritz 'em with nonstick cooking spray before you dig in. It's as easy as (mud) pie!

118 Shear genius—A smoothly working pair of pruners makes trimming a breeze, so keep yours in tip-top shape by lubricating them often with a quick spray of WD-40®.

119 What a sap—When sticky sap builds up on your pruner's blades, wipe it away with a cloth that's been moistened with isopropyl alcohol (it'll also help disinfect the blades, so you don't spread diseases among your plants).

Fast Formula

Wipe your tools' wooden handles down with this handle saver about once a month to keep 'em in fine fettle.

1 part white vinegar
1 part boiled linseed oil
1 part turpentine

Mix the ingredients in a glass jar with a tight-fitting lid. Pour some on an old cotton sock, and rub it up and down the handle until the whole thing is covered. After 10 minutes, repeat the treatment. Wait another 10 minutes, then wipe any excess off with a clean, dry cloth. Store the formula in a cool, dark place and it'll keep indefinitely.

120 **Handle the rough stuff**—To smooth out splintery wooden handles, sand them lightly with a piece of fine sandpaper or steel wool. After the splinters are gone, rub the handles down with my handle saver Fast Formula (on page 31) to condition the wood, make it less brittle, and help it last longer.

121 **Rust removal**—If your trusty trowel or shovel get rusty, grab a piece of steel wool and scrub the corrosion away. Rinse the tool off, dry it thoroughly, and give it a light coating of oil (cooking, motor, or WD-40®) to keep the rust from coming back. And to prevent rust in the first place, don't leave your tools out where they'll get wet.

122 **Looking sharp!**—Learning to sharpen tools takes practice, but even a crude job will make yard tools slice better. So grab a whetstone or file, and secure a dull tool in place with a vise or clamp. Wearing sturdy gloves, place the sharpener at a slight angle to the blade, and push it upward. Always work in the same direction along the entire edge.

For a Fantastic Finish...

To keep yard tools free from rust, make a protective sandpit. Start by filling a 5-gallon pail about 2/3 of the way full of sand, and then mix in 1/2 quart of motor oil (used is fine). Set it in a corner, and after working hard in your yard, plunge your tools up and down in the bucket a few times. The sand will scrub off dirt and rust, and the oil will give the metal a light coat of protection.

You can leave the tools in the bucket until you need them, or wipe the sand off and hang 'em up where they belong.

Got gunked up gutters?
Cruddy chrome faucets and fixtures?
Or a dehumidifier that steams things up?

Don't despair; all you need is a few of the terrific tips and tricks you'll discover inside to help you clean 'em up for years of more efficient use and service.

In this jam-packed Booklet, you'll find all sorts of super solutions to bust the dust, defy the dirt, and get rid of the grime. That way, your stuff will be ready, willing, and rarin' to go. You'll find out how to:

- **Make bathtub soap scum scram with *baking soda***
- **Keep your camera lens crystal clear with a *paintbrush***
- ***Sock* it to your ceiling fan to swipe it clean**
- **De-grime your baseball cap in your *dishwasher***
- **Sprinkle *salt* to make oven spill clean-up a breeze**
- **Keep mud off garden tools with *cooking oil* spray**
- **Plus much, much more!**

From air conditioners to waffle irons, and electric mixers to pool toys, we've got you covered. The Fast Formulas, Fantastic Finishes, and Safe & Sound ideas are just what you need to get your grubby goods looking better than new. So Clean It Up!—the fast, fun, and easy Jerry Baker way.

ABOUT JERRY BAKER...

Jerry Baker, America's #1 home and garden expert and fix-it specialist, has written over 50 books, including the bestsellers *Backyard Problem Solver, Kitchen Counter Cures*, and *Supermarket Super Products!* All of Jerry's books are jam-packed full of old-time advice, down-home wisdom, and the best remedies on earth. For more of his amazing tips, tricks, and tonics, visit Jerry online at:

www.jerrybaker.com

P.O. Box 1001, Wixom, MI 48393

I#92243395